Internet Business Success
For Software Developers

How To Grow A Profitable Online Business Using The Skills You
Already Have
By Jonathan Middaugh

You Should Read This Book If You...

1. ...want to build an online business but don't know how (I will give you a detailed business model)
2. ...are worried about having enough ideas for topics or content (I will give you a system for creating an unlimited amount of ideas)
3. ...want to build an online code portfolio to boost your career prospects (I will give you the methods to do so quickly, effectively, and with high visibility)

I will show you exactly how I:

- Quickly get my content to rank in Google searches
- Link multiple lines of business and grow revenue exponentially
- Never run out of content to create
- Have a diversified business that is resilient to competition and online trends
- Become a better software developer through growing my business

Contents

Chapter 1: An EXACT Business Model

It is hard to know what will finally motive us to stop delaying dreams, achieve something great, and be satisfied with our creative pursuits. For me, it was fear. The fear of a pandemic-driven downturn in the software development job market drove me to take action.

Initially, I simply wanted to play some defense, build a software portfolio I could reference in an interview, and have peace of mind. I was willing to hustle so I would stand out in a crowd of unemployed and anxious job applicants. I didn't know that hustle would turn into a passion that I could build a business out of.

I think many software developers are capable of creating an online business, it would mesh well with their day jobs, and they would discover a new passion. However, so many people simply don't know how to start a business. Or they think it will take too much time. Or they are embarrassed to tell anyone about their ambition. Or maybe they are afraid to fail. They need a mentor and a guide.

In this book, I lay out the EXACT business model I use to generate income online. Having a business opens the door to opportunity, serendipity, and exponential growth. I believe any software developer, data scientist, designer, etc. can use the model I use and create an internet business that will grow organically and pay out growing streams of income.

When I say an EXACT business model, I mean that I will give exact topic examples for articles, show stats from my actual articles, and list products that can be created and sold as new lines of business. The underlying business is simply this: create a central "hub" of articles on Medium.com that generate organic google traffic. Use this google traffic to link to other businesses and products that branch off from this central hub. James Altucher calls this the "Spoke and Wheel Model", but I like to think of the "Wheel" as a core "Hub".

The business that I created is centered around software development topics and looks like this:

- Medium.com Articles (hub that generates organic Google traffic) – This is even monetized a little through Medium's paywall
- eBooks on Amazon or Gumroad (spoke 1) – Monetized through sales and Amazon KDP Select borrows
- Affiliate Links (spoke 2) – Monetized through commission on ANY product a person buys from Amazon within 24 hours of clicking an affiliate link
- YouTube Channel (spoke 3) – Monetized through affiliate links and (eventually) advertisement
- Video Courses, i.e. Udemy (spoke 4) – higher priced offers than eBooks, but contain similar content
- Personal Website, i.e. a blog (spoke 5) – After proving yourself on Medium, you can grow an email list, host product landing pages, get consulting gigs, and more from your site.

The "Spoke and Wheel" model is commonly practiced online; however, I will give you an EXACT format that you can use if you are a software developer. All you have to supply is the hard work, late nights, sleepless anticipation, and willingness to be disappointed when an article doesn't do as well as expected...All jokes aside, most people who want to have an online business or presence are willing to work hard but are intimidated by not having a plan. This book will solve that.

Here is an example of the kind of detail I will offer in this book:

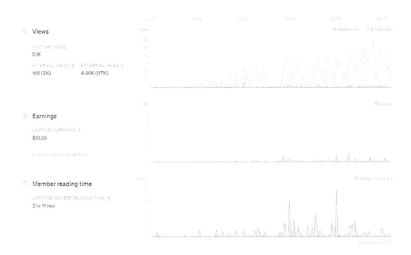

These are stats from one of my Medium.com articles, "Override TextField Border Color for Different States in Material UI". I will answer questions such as

- Why use Medium.com as a platform?
- Why do the daily views on this article grow over time (I don't market the article, and spoiler alert, views grow because Google likes it. I will tell you how to write more articles Google likes and go through exact exercises where we'll come up with some)
- How does this article earn consistently from Medium? Does this article earn money in other ways not shown here?
- How do I use articles like this to link to other spokes in my hub-and-spoke model?

Throughout this book, I offer dozens of precise guidelines on how to create a long-term and internet business. There are many ways that you can have success with an online business, but if you follow these guidelines and supply a healthy dose of persistence you WILL succeed. At a minimum, commit to six months of writing weekly Medium articles.

Chapter 2: The Hub – Medium.com

Medium is your free, passive, and infinite marketing machine for the spokes of your business

The biggest problem new internet entrepreneurs face is simply *how to be found.* Medium.com solves this for you.

Medium is a blogging platform for those who want to focus on content above all else. There is almost no overhead or setup. Even monetization is as simple as checking a box.

I use a simple strategy with Medium: write good technical articles that 1) solve a problem that others need solved or 2) demonstrate examples of how to create animations, use code libraries, etc. that people want to see. Google ranks Medium articles strongly in search results, ensuring I get traffic to my articles. From the articles, I link to relevant products (usually that I created) with affiliate links. That's the hub-and-spoke business in a nutshell.

Traffic Hacking

There are two all-important reasons to use Medium as a platform: 1) you will largely avoid the "Google Sandbox", and 2) your articles will outrank competitor articles in organic search.

The Google Sandbox is the time that a new blog or website must languish alone in the dark with essentially no Google traffic being directed to it. In other words, no one will find your business. This period lasts somewhere around six months, but even afterwards you will get less traffic than an authoritative website like Medium (I have directly tested this).

How do I know that you will avoid the Google Sandbox? Simple experience. I started with a blog, syndicated the same articles to Medium, and guess what? Before long, my Medium articles were returned in search results. My blog articles are still somewhere in oblivion, as far as Google is concerned.

Medium has also optimized its site to rank well with Google. It has high domain authority, which you will leverage to make your articles rank higher than competitor articles. Take a look at the following images from a keyword research tool called Ubersuggest:

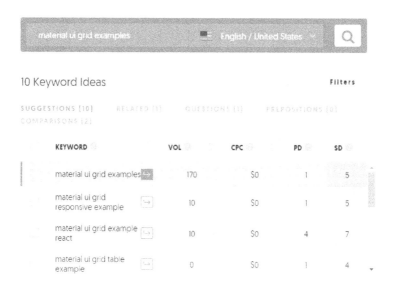

material ui grid examples   English / United States

10 Keyword Ideas   Filters

SUGGESTIONS [10]   RELATED [1]   QUESTIONS [1]   PREPOSITIONS [0]
COMPARISONS [2]

KEYWORD	VOL	CPC	PD	SD
material ui grid examples	170	$0	1	5
material ui grid responsive example	10	$0	1	5
material ui grid example react	10	$0	4	7
material ui grid table example	0	$0	1	4

Keyword Overview: material ui grid examples

 The average web page that ranks in the top 10 has 10 backlinks and a domain score of 83.

	GOOGLE SERP	EST. VISITS	LINKS	DS	SOCIAL SHARES
2	blog.logrocket...	27	23	78	0
3	dmcinfo.com/la...	16	0	54	0
4	medium.com/b...	11	0	98	0

The Medium.com article is the 4th highest result and has a DS (Domain Score) of 98 out of 100! This is incredibly high. For context, at the time of writing this book the Material-UI docs themselves have a domain score of 83. Stack Overflow has a domain score of 95.

Experiment: I made my blog the primary for the well-performing article shown below. My blog received about one-third the Google traffic for the same article as Medium. That's why the Medium traffic disappeared for a few weeks in the screenshot below.

There are other (non-Google) traffic benefits to using Medium. Medium has an internal viewer base, internal publications that can promote your articles, and curation and algorithms for pushing content to internal viewers.

Medium is really a blogging platform with a splash of social media. Good writers gain followers, and followers get notified when their followed writers publish an article. Medium also internally 'curates' articles, publishing preferred articles to 'topics' such as JavaScript and Programming.

Publications are essentially marketing machines for writers. A publication has followers in Medium as well as other social media outlets like Twitter and Facebook. A writer submits an article to a publication, and if the publication approves the article, the publication will promote it.

Here are the stats on an article about Material Table (a React data table library) that I ran in a large publication called Better Programming:

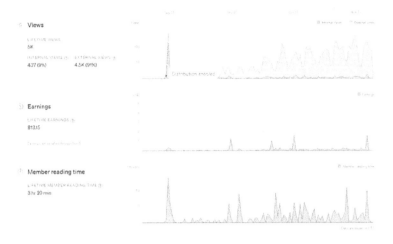

Views

LIFETIME VIEWS
5K

INTERNAL VIEWS   EXTERNAL VIEWS
437 (9%)   4.5K (91%)

Distribution enabled

Earnings

LIFETIME EARNINGS
$13.15

Member reading time

LIFETIME MEMBER READING TIME
3 hr 20 min

You can see the initial spike where it was published in Better Programming. The "Distribution enabled" badge means it was also curated by Medium.

This was all well and good. Most writers pursue this path on Medium. I do NOT. There are rules to play by when you publish in a publication, and the rules have opportunity cost (I'll tell you more in a minute).

The bump from the publication was a one-time event. For the month after that, not much happened. Then Google found the article and slowly ramped up its exposure.

Take a look at the below stats:

VIEWS BY TRAFFIC SOURCE	5K
Internal ⑦	9%
External referrals	91%
google.com	3.8K
email, IM, and direct	526
www.bing.com	65
duckduckgo.com	49
twitter.com	24
9wpgc.csb.app	20
RSS readers (full text)	10
search.yahoo.com	8
youtube.com	4
facebook.com	3
All other external referrals	25

Over three quarters of the traffic to the article has come from organic Google traffic, not from internal Medium views or marketing from the publication. This ratio will only grow over time.

So what opportunity was lost? The chance to have affiliate links, email list links, and landing page links in the article.

Medium publications want to grow. They also don't want to be seen as implicitly recommending a product you sell. These are understandable reservations. I simply think that the value they offer (a one-time boost to views) is simply not worth the opportunity cost.

I think it's fine to run some articles in publications, especially when you are new to Medium. If a Medium publication rejects an article, you learn something. If a Medium publication accepts an article but it doesn't get many views, you learn something. When an article does get run, you'll likely get some views and claps. These things are very affirming.

More importantly, your publication articles can link to supporting articles that are not in any publication. The supporting articles can contain affiliate links or other business-building links.

However, Google will supply the traffic for you if you are patient. This is how Medium becomes your infinite marketing machine. And it's passive: no social media boosting required (but social media can be a strong supplement).

How to Come Up with Unlimited Content that Google Loves

This is a two-step process.
1) Have an infinite niche
2) Within your niche, solve problems or give examples (aka, things people search for).

Step one: an infinite niche is any topic that either always has new content being created (and old content becoming obsolete), or a topic that has unlimited examples that can be imagined. Software development is replete with infinite niches.

For example, I focus on JavaScript libraries (usually libraries that use React). It is infinite because there always new libraries coming out, new problems solved, libraries to compare and contrast and so on. It is niche enough that my Medium followers (or social media followers I market content to) will care about the content I write.

Another infinite niche would be SVG animations. There is definitely interest from developers, and you can create unlimited content simply by imagining a slick new animation.

Step two: you need to write content that Google has a reason to show someone. This may seem mysterious, but I will break into actionable ideas. (I may mention software languages or libraries that you are not familiar with. They are just examples and not critical to conveying the big idea.)

First, consider your day job. What problems have you encountered where you couldn't easily google an answer? Write the article you wish you had found. For example: I needed to customize the border of a Material-UI TextField. I could not find an article that clearly explained this, so I finally figured it out and wrote a Medium article with the solution. It turns out others needed the same content; I recently had over 100 views in a day on the article. There was enough demand that I wrote a micro-eBook that dives deeper into Material-UI styling. Alternatives to this approach: create the example you wish you had found, write the setup doc you wish you had found, and so on. (As a side note: software devs spend a lot of their day googling and consuming software-related content. This means there is huge demand for blog content that solves problems which === money for us content producers.)

Second, write a cornerstone article on a popular library, then do keyword research on what problems get searched within the library. For example, I wrote an intro to Material-UI Grid component, comparing it to CSS Grid and Bootstrap. Next, I used Ubersuggest and looked at what was commonly search that didn't have a good solution on already written. Item alignment in Material-UI Grids ranked well and the top search results didn't really address the problem. The Material-UI Grid cornerstone article took maybe 10 hours to write; the MUI Grid Item Align article took about two hours.

In a later chapter I'll show you how to user Ubersuggest (which currently has a free version that will likely meet your needs) and understand keyword research. Together, we'll take a deeper look at the process I described above for Material-UI Grid and also go through the keyword research process with an animation library called Framer Motion.

Make sure every article you write was either challenging to you (you learned something and it took persistence to write) *or* you did adequate research and identified low-hanging keywords to write about. If an article doesn't meet either of these standards, there's a good chance it won't get much traffic. Figuring out what topics will do well is a skill, but the tools in this book will start you a few levels up.

You can view any article mentioned from this book if you want example of how to write articles that get Google traffic. There is a link to each article in the Resources section at the end of the book.

Search Traffic Tailwinds

Let's say in your first month of creating your own hub-and-spoke internet business you enthusiastically write 10 Medium articles and....nothing from Google. Do Not Be Afraid!

Here's a look at some of my traffic results, for context:

Intro to Material-UI Grid:

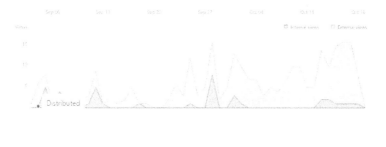

VIEWS BY TRAFFIC SOURCE   269

Internal ⑦   15%

External referrals   85%

google.com   184

email, IM, and direct   35

www.bing.com   5

duckduckgo.com   4

qwant.com   1

This article was only about a month old when this screenshot was taken. You can see the slow progress as Google is returning the article more and more often in search results. Here's the same article after a second month:

Views

LIFETIME VIEWS
738

INTERNAL VIEWS   EXTERNAL VIEWS
66 (9%)   672 (91%)

Notice the exponential growth. This is completely the result of Google search traffic.

JSS Selectors:

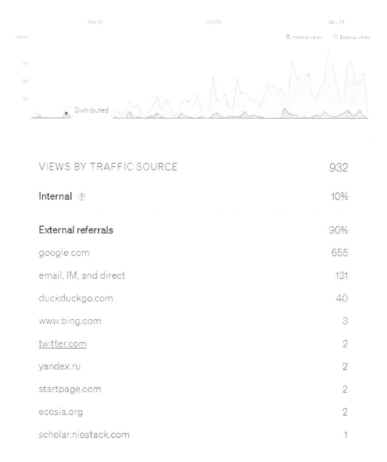

VIEWS BY TRAFFIC SOURCE	932
Internal ⑦	10%
External referrals	90%
google.com	655
email, IM, and direct	131
duckduckgo.com	40
www.bing.com	3
twitter.com	2
yandex.ru	2
startpage.com	2
ecosia.org	2
scholar.niostack.com	1

I expect this article will be quite a niche topic. Nevertheless, the traffic grows weekly.

MobX @computed:

Sometimes Google will not direct much traffic to an article for months, then decide it is a good search result.

These were examples from articles that I consider moderately successful. Even my best articles have been growing for months and still are on an uptrend of views. The point is you can't rule an article out based on the first 60 days of results. It is both alarming to know that your articles' success depends on a Google algorithm, and yet exciting to know that there are tens of thousands of searches for some of these topics, and your articles may become one of the top results and see incredible traffic.

A case in point: I got about 3k article views in August 2020, and 6k views in September 2020. This was despite only publishing two new articles in September, which added less than 200 views that month. I had spent my time writing another eBook instead of Medium articles. However, Google was propelling me forward through organic search traffic. (I do recommend publishing regularly...if you have a website, regular posting may increase Google's domain strength rating for the site. The same may be true for your suite of articles published under your Medium profile.)

There are other tailwinds. Consider this scenario: you write a suite of articles on an up-and-coming animation library. Then next year, the library is the top choice for several large companies and suddenly your articles are seeing thousands of views per month.

This is a business with lots of serendipity. I suspect I have received additional views at times from Medium because a well-known tech author wrote a post on a library I had articles about, then Medium recommended my articles to readers of the other author's post.

The articles I write are micro-assets with potential that gets unlocked over the course of months or years.

So Many Ways to Make Money from Medium

The articles (micro-assets) I write have several routes for making money using Medium as the hub.

First, Medium is directly monetized via paying members. Medium has a $5 monthly subscription fee (at the time of this writing). A portion of this fee is then divided up and distributed to every author that the member read an article from. The more time that a Medium member spends on my article, the bigger cut I get from that $5.

There are two interesting pieces to this. First, Medium calculates daily how much an article earned the previous day. But the $5 gets divided over the month. This tells me there is an estimation algorithm involved. Second, sometimes my articles make money on days when non-members read the article but no Medium member read it. This is because Medium pays a bounty if someone becomes a member shortly after reading your article.

The potential for earning money directly from Medium means it could be considered a business spoke. However, I don't view it that way simply because I think Medium's value lies in its potential for marketing your other assets: eBooks, courses, and so on.

For example, and this is just my particular experience, I make about 10X as much from selling eBooks as I do from Medium. I make almost as much in affiliate commission (basically free money) as I do from Medium. I don't have advertising yet on my YouTube channel, but I estimate that advertising rates will be about 5X higher per YouTube view than Medium view. However, Medium drives most of my traffic to my YouTube channel, and significant traffic to my eBooks. It is a crucial center for my business model.

Before moving on, I think it is important to mention that software developers live all around the world. If you are running a blog instead of using Medium, and if you rely on digital ad revenue instead of Medium monetization, you will see low ad revenue per view. This is because many views come from parts of the world where advertisers don't pay as much per view. For example, views and clicks from United States residents cost an advertiser more than views from just about anywhere else in the world. If only 25% of your views are from the U.S., don't compare your results to the ad revenue from a personal finance blog where 80% of views are US viewers.

Also, some of these views don't have potential for affiliate link commission. For example, I can sell an eBook on the Amazon store in India, but I can't get an affiliate commission for the click unless I have a bank account in India. It's simply a rule Amazon (or India) imposes.

Medium Miscellaneous

A few straightforward steps for optimizing your Medium business.

1. If you follow my business model, you need a "Call to Action" in your article for selling eBooks, courses, whatever.

   Here is an example of a link to a landing page for a product or email signup list. It is at the bottom of an article and makes use of a separator:

. . .

Get developer-specific side hustle tips from me here.

Here's another example, but this time I paused in the middle of the article to mention a relevant resource (an eBook that dives deeper into the topic). Notice the required disclosure of the affiliate link:

There are more examples below, but if you want to gain an in-depth understanding of Material-UI syntax and APIs for styling components, I recommend you read my book, Styling Material-UI Components (affiliate link). I cover the class object API, Styled Components, and overriding components using the theme. Furthermore, there are many more examples of custom component styling.

2. If you also use YouTube as a business spoke, I highly recommend linking to the YouTube video at the top of your Medium post. First, I believe YouTube will monetize better so it's fine if traffic goes there instead. More importantly, some article viewers may be out of free views for the month (Medium lets anyone read three articles per month for free). If your YouTube link is at the top of the article, it is possible that a non-member gets to see enough of your article to click the YouTube link.

3. Always have a resources section with links to relevant code, YouTube videos you created, and third-party articles you reference.
4. You MUST give credit for images. Unsplash and Pixabay are common resources for free images. Make sure to include a credit in the image text.
5. If you have a blog and syndicate the articles to Medium, make sure you tell Google which is the "original" source and should be returned in search results. Do this by setting a "canonical link" in the non-primary article. In my business model, I make sure Medium is primary, so each blog post gets marked with a canonical link pointing to my "original" Medium post.
6. Someday Google may decide that Medium does not deserve such a high Domain Score. Google updates their algorithms regularly. The multiple spokes that I discuss are not just a way to increase revenue; they also reduce risk. First, after you have proven your persistence in this business by writing 20 articles or so, I think it's a great idea to have a blog that has all the articles canonically contained on it. If Google downgrades Medium, you can set your blog as primary. Second, the other business spokes all have internal search. YouTube, Amazon, and Udemy all have internal algorithms for helping buyers and viewers find content. My point is that you are building a resilient business and will overcome any difficulties.
7. There are alternative platforms to Medium, such as Substack. You could build a similar business on another platform. However, I think Medium currently has advantages in terms of size and Google ranking.
8. Social Media Promotion: if you create your own publication, you can create a following on whatever social media platform you desire simply from the organic traffic to your publication. Medium includes the easily embedded links below.

Some people grow massive audiences directly through social media engagement. That is a lucrative strategy for many, and it could easily be combined with the SEO-focused strategy of this book. Affiliate links and product promotion to an engaged social media audience can be an extraordinarily lucrative opportunity. It simply takes a little extra time and effort. I recommend building up a strong business hub on Medium and developing several premium products before strongly pursuing a social media strategy. The simple reasons are that good content creates a strong core and you should develop your voice and focus as a business before pushing content to an audience.

Chapter 3: eBooks – Spoke 1

In the hub-and-spoke model, we get traffic and prove our value with free content on Medium. To truly monetize the hub, we must convert some portion of the viewers into purchasers of our premium content.

I believe a paid eBook is the most natural next step from a Medium article. Medium article viewers already are willing to consume content in written form and they are interested in the topic. Additionally, if you are capable of writing a 1,500 word Medium article, you can dive deeper and write a 15,000 word eBook on the topic. Best of all, someday you may get to say "I wrote a book on that" in an interview!

In this discussion I'll use Amazon as an example publishing platform because that's where I have self-published and I have had a good experience.

What is a Book, Really?

An eBook is whatever you want it to be. I have written a "microbook" that could have just been a long Medium post. I have written several books that are study guides or prep, for example "300 JavaScript Interview Mastery Questions". And I have even written a couple of financial books that are a more traditional format.

Self-publishing platforms do not significantly regulate the style or content of eBooks. Instead, it comes down to customer reviews. Create content that helps people, market it accurately, and you will make sales.

I recommend writing at least 20 Medium articles before you write your first eBook. This allows you to experiment in a lower risk environment...meaning that you won't sink three months into a product no one wants. If you write 20 Medium articles on programming topics in your infinite niche, you will likely have some search traffic, some article stats to compare, and a general idea of what problems people are trying to solve.

Example: The microbook I mentioned is a "how-to" on styling Material-UI, a JavaScript component library. I knew from work that it was difficult to find good answers on this topic. Furthermore, an article I wrote on styling Material-UI Textboxes was getting lots of traffic. Therefore, I had 1) validation that there was interest in the book and 2) a traffic generator where I could link to my book.

Another approach is to aggregate the content from multiple Medium articles and repurpose/repackage it as a book. Even though people may be able to access your Medium articles, this is valuable for several reasons: First, you organize the content for them, and second, people searching internally in Amazon (or whatever publisher) will find your content organically. If you do this, make sure to comply with the rules of Amazon KDP Select, which I'll get to shortly.

If you have a book topic idea that did not come from your Medium experience, consider the following for validation. First, check the competition on Amazon and weigh that against the size of the demand for the topic. For example, my Docker Certified Associate study guide does better than my JavaScript interview study guide. Likely this is because there is far more competition among JavaScript books than Docker study guides. Second, write an article with free content first. Before I wrote my JavaScript book, I wrote an article called "50 Difficult JavaScript Interview Questions". This helped me to evaluate search traffic potential. If you publish a book in a competitive niche, you can still do well if you drive your own traffic to your book.

The books I have mentioned so far have been highly technical and are best linked to from Medium articles with related content. There is another type of book that you need in your arsenal for generating paid revenue: Anchor Content.

Anchor content includes evergreen meta topics such as: interviewing, negotiating, health, finances, business building, and humor. An example book title that many developers would be curious about: "2X your Salary in 2 Years Through Negotiation". I highly recommend that you write at least one anchor book if you pursue a hub-and-spoke business model. The anchor book gives you the following benefits:

- It can be a premium priced product
- You can link to it from any article if you do not have a more relevant product to link to
- It can be relevant for many years without being updated
- It can be a flagship product that establishes your personal brand
- It is an opportunity to branch out into less technical content while remaining relevant to your niche

Here are two pro tips I have learned from writing books. 1) Make sure the content at the beginning is excellent because this will be previewed. For example, the first 10 questions in a study guide should be some of the best. 2) Make an outline of all the chapters and subheadings. Then the book will write itself. Keep a notepad or note taking app handy so you do not lose a single idea. I use Trello.com for this, and I will have more info on this excellent tool later.

All About Amazon

I have traditionally only sold my eBooks through Amazon for the following key reasons:

- The affiliate program is lucrative

- It has its own internal search traffic and people are there wanting to buy things
- It was easy to set up my first eBook in 2014 and the process has not changed much. It is friendly to both first-time and experienced authors

However, two new areas I recently explored are paperback and audiobook. With Amazon, it is simple to create an eBook and then create and link a paperback and audio version. Buyers expect these items to be priced higher, and so the eBook is perceived as a "value". Even better, there is demand for paperback and audio, and they often have a higher net royalty than an equivalent eBook.

Amazon has a print-on-demand service for paperback books so you have no hassle; they handle printing and shipping. You upload the content similarly to the eBook content. Be sure to include links in a paperback-friendly way, and if possible, edit the book in such a way to keep page count lower to reduce printing costs.

Deciding which content platform to use is a hotly debated topic on the internet. Two other potential options for technical books are Packt and Gumroad. The main benefit of Packt is that it is focused on technical books. However, it has a royalty structure that may be more suited to authors certain to sell in the thousands of copies yearly.

Gumroad is an interesting competitor to Amazon for two reasons: they take a much smaller royalty cut and they pay far more quickly. Their royalty cut is 8.5% + $0.30 per sale at the time of this writing, but this is subject to change. Compare this to Amazon: Amazon takes either a whopping 65% (for books less than $2.99 or more than $9.99) or 30% for books in the sweet spot in between. Gumroad then pays every Friday for the prior week's earnings. This means if you make a sale, you wait between 7 and 14 days to get the money. Amazon on the other hand pays monthly, and you don't get your money for two to three months. For example, Amazon book sales in January pay at the end of March.

After reading that comparison, you may be wondering why I use Amazon (I'm wondering too!). Amazon has a marketing program called Amazon KDP Select that requires content to be exclusive to Amazon. Once again, it is hotly debated whether this is good or bad for authors, but it works like this: if I publish a book and choose to include it in KDP Select, then Amazon Prime members can read it for free. There is a pot of money that gets divided up at the end of the month amongst all KDP Select books, and I get a bigger cut based on how many pages were read for free in my KDP Select books. I still can make sales to non-prime members.

I also get the benefit of being able to run regular KDP Select deals where the book can be sold for free or at a reduced price. Here's the two-fold reason KDP Select can be a strong benefit: 1) for new authors, it likely boosts their book in internal Amazon search, and 2) if I have a strong email list/twitter following/etc, I can do a KDP Select countdown deal and pitch an affiliate link to my audience. This gets me increased sales plus affiliate commissions on other products my audience members might buy.

A few more details on Amazon KDP Select: in the past Amazon reserved the right to change the price of eBooks in the program. I do not know if this is currently in effect. Also, be careful in how you repackage content from Medium for an eBook if the eBook is in KDP Select. KDP Select requires content to be original to Amazon, so make sure it is new and value-adding. Finally, KDP Select makes it easy to participate in Prime day and other seasonal deals.

When you are starting out, it is difficult to know what the right strategy is. However, experimenting is easy. For example, I can include a book in KDP Select on a month-to-month basis. This could allow me to try KDP Select for a couple of months, then drop it and try Amazon (without KDP Select) and Gumroad simultaneously. There are also an abundance of metrics and tools for collecting metrics. If you are running an internet business while you "still have a day job", you have an opportunity to learn with low risk. And by the way, Gumroad has an affiliate program as well, so try things out and see what brings in the most revenue.

Details of Creating and Uploading the Book

Writing an eBook requires only a few more processing steps than writing a typical paper.

I get my covers created professionally on Fiver.com. Go with a highly rated vendor. They usually are willing to do quite a bit of back-and-forth to create the perfect cover for you. Have them create a paperback and audio cover for a little higher price.

If I include a paperback book on Amazon, I set the dimensions to 6"x9" per Amazon's recommendation. I also make sure to check that the formatting of any code in the book looks good at this size. Finally, make sure links are presented in a paperback-friendly way. Do not embed links in the eBook text and forget to change that for paperback.

This is the url for publishing on Amazon: kdp.amazon.com. The KDP in the url stands for Kindle Direct Publishing. Create an account, and Amazon will step you through the rest. If you get stuck, there are lots of websites and forums to turn to for help. However, I think Amazon did a good job of making their publishing site simple to use.

The most important third-party tool for selling your books is geniuslink.com. Consider this: what happens if you publish your book in multiple Amazon markets (i.e. the US, UK, Germany, etc.), but you can only embed one link in a Medium post? You want your Medium readers to click through to the version of your book that is in the appropriate marketplace for them. This is where GeniusLink comes in: through their site you create one link to an Amazon product, and their site directs viewers to the appropriate international Amazon marketplace. In other words, if a German reader clicks a GeniusLink in Medium, they will be directed to the applicable product in the German marketplace. GeniusLink also syncs with any applicable Amazon affiliate IDs you register. This tool is inexpensive and in my business it pays for itself. I cover it more in depth in the chapter on affiliate links.

Here is my series of habits for getting a book written: After making an outline of the book, I evaluate how much total content there is. I set an aggressive schedule, i.e. write 20 questions a day for my "300 JavaScript Interview Mastery Questions" book. I look at the calendar and see how many **weekdays** it will take me to finish the book, assuming I hit my daily commitment. I leave Saturdays for editing and catching up (or getting ahead), and Sundays I take the day off. I work a full-time job, so I write an hour in the morning and an hour in the evening (do what works for you). In the example of my JavaScript interview book, at 20 questions per day it took me 15 days to finish. Thinking "15 days to a finished book!" is far easier psychologically than "Only 300 questions left." The same practice can be done for chapter books like this one: generate an outline of titles and sections, commit to a certain amount per day, and mark on your calendar the day you will finish. If you stick to this practice, you will do what most people do not: You will finish.

A last note - Make sure you do good editing of the book. My personal struggle is to finish writing and be excited to launch, so I slack off with editing. However, doing 99% percent of the work but getting a bad review for formatting issues is not a good way to grow a business. Protect the asset you created by making sure it is high quality.

Chapter 4: Affiliate Links – Spoke 2

For some internet businesses, the entire business is built around creating a traffic driver (the hub) and then using affiliate links to link to recommended 3rd party products. Given the power and earnings potential, I believe affiliate commissions should be examined as their own spoke in the online business that you create.

Show Me the (Free) Money

Amazon has probably the most widely known affiliate program. If a person clicks on a link to an Amazon product, and the link has your tracking ID, you will get a commission from anything the person buys from Amazon in the next 24 hours. This is tracked through a browser cookie. There are a few caveats, for example if the person clicks someone else's link after yours then you lose the commission opportunity.

Growing affiliate link revenue is simply about getting the link in front of as many viewers as possible and linking to the most relevant item. Affiliate commissions are a perfect fit for the high organic search traffic business model we are pursuing.

Currently, all my links are to eBooks I have written. I see about 2%-3% of traffic to my Medium articles click my Amazon affiliate links. Of those that click, 10%-15% buy my book *or* another product for which I receive commission. Be aware that it can be difficult to filter out the clicks from web crawler bots and the clicks from actual humans.

For each eBook I sell, I receive a 4% commission. For each paperback, I receive a 4.5% commission. Paperbacks usually are priced higher to cover printing costs, so it is always exciting when one sells through an affiliate link. I have made as little as $0.04 from an affiliate link purchase, and as much as $2.43

when an $80+ item (not my product) was purchased with my tracking ID active.

As good as the affiliate fees are, the bounties may be the real money maker. Amazon pays out bounties when a person signs up for a program (like Amazon Prime or Kindle Unlimited) after clicking your link. Part of the reason I usually have my eBooks available in KDP Select is because it encourages people to sign up for Kindle Unlimited when they see they could read my book for free if they were an Unlimited member. The bounty as of writing this book is $3 per signup. To date, I have made more from bounties than from affiliate sales commission.

Keep in mind that software developers live all around the world. U.S. residents have relatively high incomes compared to many places. With that said, most clicks result in no revenue, but some result in quite a bit. My total estimate of what I earn from Amazon's affiliate program, averaged out across all clicks from all countries: $0.05 per click. You will certainly see a different average, depending on your strategy and skill with affiliate marketing.

Unfortunately, Amazon lowered its affiliate program commission rates in early 2020. The default rate is 4%, but the range is 1% to 10% depending on the type of item sold. I have linked to the commission chart in the resources section. The affiliate rates are set by Amazon and subject to change.

Maximize the Money

Now that we have discussed the potential of affiliate links, we need cover some technical aspects of maximizing affiliate revenue.

First: register for appropriate international Amazon affiliate accounts. For example, if you sell copies of your eBook in the UK, Germany, Canada, etc. you should consider registering for an affiliate account for each country. It only takes a few minutes to register, and it is a good way to pick up a little extra income. Keep in mind that Amazon lets account creators choose what language the signup page displays in.

I mentioned geniuslink.com when discussing eBooks, but we need to discuss its value for affiliate marketing. Here is an example: You create an eBook and publish it in several international Amazon markets, and you also have Amazon Affiliate accounts in several of those markets. It seems like a lot of links to keep track of, but GeniusLink takes the pain out of it. All of that condenses down to one link; GeniusLink handles routing and assignment of the appropriate affiliate ID.

Here is why GeniusLink is critical: I took this screenshot of GeniusLink's world mapping of where my clicks came from in the previous 30 days. The US is the single largest source of clicks for me, and yet only 17% of the clicks on my links came from the US. Considering I only embed one text link and one image link per article, I would miss out on over 80% of my click traffic.

I will condense it down even more: most months my eBooks make more than half their sales outside the US. My affiliate income is about evenly split between the US and the rest of the world. GeniusLink, at the time of writing this, only costs $5 per month for their starting plan. 3rd party tools should pay for themselves, and GeniusLink certainly does for me.

Creating a link to a product on Amazon is snappy in the Amazon Affiliate site. Go to the Product Linking tab and simply search for your product (or a third-party product). I like to make both text-based links and image links. If you have a sharp cover design for your book, use the image for an image-based affiliate link. Usually at the bottom of my Medium articles, I write a sentence or two about my applicable eBook (with a text-based link in the paragraph), then insert the image-based affiliate link directly below.

Keep Experimenting

Internet Businesses have massive opportunity for analytics and optimization because everything is digital. Experiments are worth the price.

For example, I make clones of links in GeniusLink and use them in different ways to experiment with what draws more clicks. Each link has metrics and tracking in GeniusLink, and I can use these analytics to determine optimum link placement, text, and so on. I can also create different Amazon affiliate links to track clicks.

Experiment with where links are placed, the text around them, using images as links, and using email and social media to push links to your audience.

You may be one tweak away from boosting affiliate earnings or product sales by 20% (or 200%!). You only learn by doing. Expect that the first six months of working you will make lots of mistakes. Money will trickle in slowly. Eventually you will master systems and processes that work for you.

Take the business model demonstrated in this book and experiment with it. A natural progression for your internet business might be like mine: create a hub of Medium articles for traffic, create an eBook, then link to it with affiliate links. However, while you are building up your Medium portfolio, consider linking to 3rd party eBooks, digital courses, or other products *if* you have verified they are high quality. I recommend this for two reasons: you get some experience at what kinds of links drive traffic, and you might even see some revenue (which is highly motivating).

Another twist on this strategy: write an article that has the potential for a follow-up eBook and start out by linking to an existing 3rd party product with great reviews (maybe you have purchased and read it and can recommend it). The affiliate link revenue may be good enough that you choose not to create your own product. You potentially maximize your revenue and save time to pursue other opportunities with your hub-and-spoke business.

Chapter 5: YouTube – Spoke 3

YouTube is like Medium: it has organic search, it has its own monetization system, and it can contain affiliate links to your products. In my hub-and-spoke model, why is YouTube a spoke and not the hub? Because Medium is a great hack for getting significant view count to a new YouTube channel.

YouTube has powerful organic search potential. First, YouTube has internal search: viewers will use the search bar at the top of YouTube to find content. Also, Google searches can and do return video as part of the results. Furthermore, Google search queries can be designed to return *only* videos. Finally, Google owns YouTube and is friendly to returning YouTube content in Google searches.

I find that the "Google Sandbox" seems to be shorter for YouTube than for a personal blog or website. There is a slightly higher barrier to entry since a video takes more technical knowledge (and guts) to produce.

Strategy Session

The combination of Medium + YouTube is an even greater opportunity for traffic. My strategy is simple: after I create a Medium article, I create a video that covers the same content. I then link to the video from the Medium article. I have already discussed the power of Medium in Google search: now I harness it to bring instant and continuous traffic to my YouTube channel.

While creating the Medium article, I have already coded the examples and written the content, so creating a video usually only takes an extra hour. To rephrase: an extra hour of effort creates an entirely new business line to generate direct income from views, plus income from affiliate links and product sales.

Furthermore, some people reading my Medium article may have a different learning style and appreciate the video. It truly is a win-win situation.

I typically place a link to the video in the text of my first paragraph in Medium. I also embed the actual video at the end of my article in a "Resources" section. I typically convert around 3%-5% of my Medium viewers to YouTube.

Each YouTube video has a description section below the video. I describe the video, link to any relevant code repositories, then link to the relevant Medium article. The link back to the Medium article ultimately gives my Medium article exposure to YouTube organic search. Finally, I add an affiliate link. Consider experimenting with the order of these links and notes: an affiliate that does not get seen will not get clicked.

Keep in mind that Medium publications do not allow affiliate links. However, your articles in publications can link to YouTube videos that you created. This means YouTube can be a backdoor for getting affiliate link clicks from your articles that are run in publications.

Growing YouTube

YouTube directly monetizes through ads. However, you need to have *both* 1000 subscribers to your channel and 4000 hours of watch time from viewers before you can monetize with ads (this is why affiliate links are critical for new channels).

Traffic from Medium will be a start for getting subscribers and watch time. In fact, if you publish enough content on a regular schedule, you likely will get to 1000 subs and 4000 hours without any other marketing. Keep in mind that the content in the business model this book recommends is very organic-search-friendly. However, there are more opportunities for driving traffic:

- Consider posting the video on Reddit. There are some subreddits that allow self-promotion such as posting video links. Just make sure you follow the subreddit's rules. Make sure to also have some engagement with other reddit readers and add value.
- Regular publishing may boost your video rankings in YouTube search. At the very least, it can't hurt. I do not create a video for all my Medium articles, but I do create a video for every cornerstone piece.
- Publish visual-friendly videos. This means coding examples, especially UI related, are searched for and do well.

Before you start creating videos, consider setting up what's known as a "Brand Channel". This is simply a channel that has a name *other than* your YouTube username. For example, I created a Medium publication called The Clever Dev simply to make my articles seem more professional. I also named my YouTube channel The Clever Dev.

This part is critical: After creating your brand channel, go to Customization > Branding and add a video watermark. This is an image that will be shown in your video that has a subscribe button. You want to make it easy for viewers to subscribe. You also want to set up other basic info about your channel, such as a description. Finally, under Settings > Channel, you can add tags so that your channel will be found more easily.

Also be careful not to overload your subscribers. If you publish too often, subscribers may drop you because you fill up their feed. When subscribers drop you, it is that much more difficult to get to 1000 subscribers for ad monetization. I do not recommend publishing more than twice per week; keep in mind this is different than Medium where a minimum follower count is not required for monetization.

One last tip: for coding videos, the audience does not have to see your face (unless you want them to). The only software and equipment I recommend is OBS Studio (free screen recording software), Canva or another tool for making thumbnails, and a pair of decent headphones with a mic (like you would use for gaming). The recipe for YouTube success is simple: use OBS to record your live coding, have good audio, and create lots and lots of content that will help people.

Chapter 6: Video Platforms – Spoke 4

Udemy, Pluralsight, LinkedIn Learning, Teachable, Skillshare, and other video platforms have proliferated in the last decade. They are popular with content creators because video products can command a strong premium over written content. Video platforms are popular with students because they add another learning avenue and will often include access to the instructor for Q&A.

Premium video content is the culmination of the other business spokes previously discussed. eBooks or YouTube videos can serve as an outline for creating a video course. Better yet, eBooks and YouTube can be used to gauge market interest in a topic. If you have an eBook with strong sales, consider converting it to a video with 5X or 10X the price.

Video platforms have other familiar characteristics: affiliate programs and internal search traffic on their platforms. Consider the affiliate program for Udemy – it currently has a 20% commission rate, your affiliate cookie lasts for 7 days, and Udemy supplies you with coupons and other promotional material. If you have strong traffic to your Medium posts, creating a video course for the premium price and strong affiliate potential can be a lucrative business.

One more thing to consider: some video platforms (like Udemy) offer video courses for sale, while others (like Pluralsight) are monthly subscription services. If you have a video on Pluralsight and someone views it, you get a cut of their monthly subscription. This may not initially sound as lucrative but consider this: thousands of companies purchase Pluralsight licenses for their software developers and encourage them to watch videos as part of their internal training package. That is a lot of dollars up for grabs.

Chapter 7: Your Own Site – Spoke 5

After you have proven your persistence in creating a strong hub of software development articles on Medium, it is time to create a simple website. You may be wondering what benefit there could be when Medium is quicker, easier, and has better SEO. However, there are things you can have on your own site that you simply cannot do on Medium:

- Product landing pages
- Mailing list landing pages
- It can qualify you for affiliate programs that do not accept a Medium portfolio
- Lead pages for consulting/coaching/etc.

When you create your own site is up to you, but I would recommend one of two milestones: *either* you have written a minimum of 20 articles on Medium, you are seeing some traffic and financial traction, and you enjoy the business, *or* you have decent traffic on Medium and would like to collect emails and direct traffic to landing pages.

Many people can waste time setting up a site instead of creating content. Ultimately, content is king. Viewers care about content that helps them far more than what theme you are using. Remember, in our business model your blog will be a business spoke, not the primary hub.

Opportunities Abound

Product landing pages help sell your products in two ways: you can link to them in Medium without including the pesky "affiliate link" disclaimer, and you can include product testimonials and other enticing promotional information for prospective buyers.

For example, in the Call-To-Action at the bottom of your Medium article, you can simply write:

> Are you a software developer interested in building an online business? Click here to learn more.

This looks much better than a direct link to a product, like this:

> Are you a software developer interested in building an online business? Click here to learn more (affiliate link).

A landing page can also create opportunities for ad campaigns. Google ad campaigns commonly link to landing pages on blogs or niche websites.

Another type of landing page is an email list landing page. If you want to create regular readership to your blog or Medium articles, or if you regularly release new premium products your audience may be interested in, you likely want to build a list of emails. Email lists can be built using a tool like MailChimp (which is free for the first 2000 emails you collect). MailChimp has a quick tool for building a landing page or widget, which can then be inserted into your blog. Then simply link to the email list landing page from Medium articles, and you will organically grow your email list.

Two final benefits of maintaining a website separate from Medium are 1) the chance to scoop up a little extra Google traffic that Medium did not pick up, and 2) the opportunity to write about topics that do not fit your Medium niche. For example, if your Medium niche is state management in JavaScript, your website might include broader articles like monthly income reports or software book reviews. These articles may be more personable or fit better with an email list. The website may be an opportunity to develop a dedicated fan base.

Medium Insurance

Truly one of the most important reasons to have your own site is in case Google reduces the domain authority of Medium.com. If Medium was no longer an option for your articles (whatever the reason), you can set your articles on your site to be the primary with Google and set the syndicated article on Medium as canonical. It is doubtful that you would get the same traffic levels, but you would still have a viable business.

With this in mind, I do recommend that you consider the following for your site:

- Do basic SEO
- Learn how to monetize through Adsense or another ad network
- Pick a theme that you like and take the time to figure out a logo and color scheme that give you a brand.

Chapter 8: Good Content Research

The core idea of this online business model is that Medium's authority with Google gives Medium articles a strong advantage in search traffic. However, you must write content that people are searching for. This raises the question: how do you know what software development-related content people are looking for? In this section, I will discuss the "how" of content research and then demonstrate with an example.

As previously mentioned, I believe there are "infinite niches" in the software engineering world. These niches are broad enough to have many people searching for related content, narrow enough to give you a specialized skillset, and infinite because there are new technologies (libraries, languages, frameworks, etc.) constantly released. For example, my infinite niche is React libraries: reviewing them, comparing them, creating examples, and solving problems in them that I could not find an answer for anywhere else.

My strategy for content research is the following:
- Pick a cornerstone topic to write an introductory or demonstration article about
    - Commonly searched phrases include "library XYZ examples" or "library ABC vs XYZ"
    - Look for cornerstone topics that have 0-3 existing Medium articles
- Extensively cover subtopics
    - Preferably specific how-to topics that have NO relevant articles covering the subject (Google will quickly pick up your article)
    - If there is at least some monthly traffic searching for the relevant subtopic keywords, it can be lucrative

This is a simple, repeatable system for generating content. Below I will explore Ubersuggest, the free SEO tool I use for validating what content is being searched for and how difficult the competition is for the topic.

Tools of the Trade

Ubersuggest has an incredible level of free functionality that has helped my internet business thrive. Look at the two screenshots below. In the first, I have entered a keyword and received a relative score on how often that keyword is searched. If there is not a zero score, I am interested.

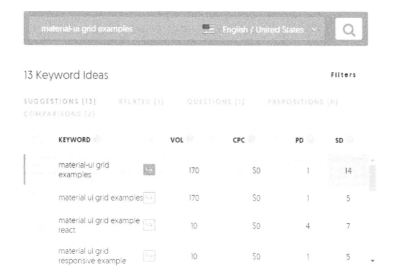

In the second, the list of Google search results is returned with links to the articles, relevant information about monthly visits, and some domain information.

Keyword Overview: material-ui grid examples

The average web page that ranks in the top 10 has 10 backlinks and a domain score of 78.

GOOGLE SERP	EST. VISITS	LINKS	DS	SOCIAL SHARES
bit.dev/mui-org...	11	0	71	0
medium.com/b...	7	0	98	2
medium.com/t...	5	0	98	0

The second Medium.com article listed is one of my articles (seventh in the Google search results, according to Ubersuggest). I do not look at this list for the stats. I look at it to see how many Medium.com articles I am competing against. Google gives Medium such a high domain score that I do not get concerned if there are dozens of competing articles outside of Medium.com.

After gathering topic ideas, I record them in an online list-making tool called Trello (many readers likely have used it). Take a look at the image:

I have a board per category. Within each board I have: To Do, Doing, and Done. I can record whatever details I want in each card. I often capture ideas in the "To Do" even if I have not validated their competition or search traffic yet. This simple system ensures I do not lose track of good ideas.

Keyword Research Examples

Here is the exact process I went through for keyword research:

I mentioned the second article in the Ubersuggest results for the "material-ui grid examples" keyword phrase was an article I wrote. It is titled "Intro to Material-UI Grid Component". It receives dozens of views every day and its week-over-week view count is growing. First, this is validation of my process: I have relatively quickly gotten an article on a well-covered topic into the first page of Google search results. Second, this is an opportunity for additional articles covering subtopics.

In writing the Material-UI Grid article, I became familiar with several technical aspects of Material-UI Grid. One is the "Item" subcomponent in the grid. My next step was to search "material-ui item" and see what suggestions Ubersuggest can give:

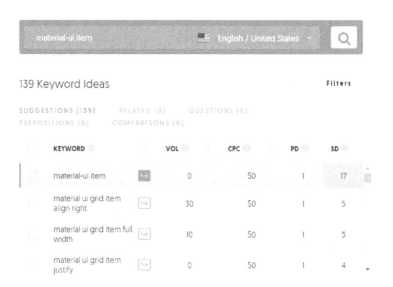

I saw "material ui grid item align right" and I knew that would be a straightforward article to write. In fact, it likely would take only a few hours. I investigated the top articles that Ubersuggest said Google would return for this keyword phrase; there was only one Medium article and it was not particularly relevant. My final step was to make a note in the relevant Trello board's "To Do" list, because Material-UI Grid Item Alignment looks like a promising topic.

Other relevant keywords I will research might be "material ui grid styling", "material ui grid nested components", "material ui grid flex", and so on. Anything about styling, common challenges, or community requested features is potentially strong topic material.

Another library that I have written about is Framer Motion, an animation library for React. I wrote a cornerstone piece, and then researched more keywords to write about. The screenshot below is another simple way to generate ideas:

G   framer motion vs

Q   framer motion vs - Google Search

Q   framer motion vs **react spring**

Q   framer motion vs **gsap**

Q   framer motion vs **react transition group**

Q   framer motion vs **spring**

Q   framer motion vs **react spring reddit**

Google will gladly show you what others are searching for, and "XYZ vs...." is a common phrase. Ubersuggest's free version has a limited daily search amount, so using this Google tactic can stretch your Ubersuggest value.

I used the above strategy to find the keyword phrase "framer motion vs react spring" and I checked it in Ubersuggest. It had decent monthly search volume and the Medium article in the top 10 search results was only about Framer Motion without any mention of React Spring. This looks like a good candidate for an article.

Keep in mind, this may feel like you are "manufacturing" content ideas. The best way to get great content ideas is to be deep in a library/language/etc. and encounter real challenges that simply have not been answered yet.

One area I stay away from: articles that have been covered hundreds of times by other Medium authors. For example, I do not recommend writing an article such as "Why You Should Use TypeScript" or "How to Clear an Array in JavaScript". At best, you might get into a publication and get a one-time view bump. However, you will not get long-term Google search traffic (unless you had absolutely the best article ever on the topic, but there is already lots of tough competition). Low competition keywords/phrases result in long-term Google traffic.

I do strongly recommend that you "consume" lots of content. Read other developer blogs, follow Medium publications on programming, follow Google announcements, and read some of the meta books of software development. Of course, write code for the sake of building things (or for work) and the ideas will come to you. Regardless of where your content ideas come from, the final step is simple: write quality articles that answer questions thoroughly or provide great examples. That is the repeatable system - create good content that you know people are looking for.

Chapter 9: Internet Business Milestones

Each article, video, eBook, or course you create is a micro asset that will exponentially impact your business. The challenge is starting and maintaining momentum early in your business. As a point of reference, I will share some of the results I have experienced.

My Personal Results Time Frame

Let's revisit some stats I've previously mentioned from my article "Override TextField Border Color for Different States in Material UI".

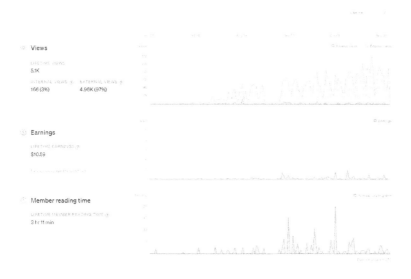

I published this article on May 29th, 2020. In June, it made a total of 14 cents. The article was in the Google sandbox that first month, I was new to writing Medium articles, and I simply had no idea what worked and what didn't.

In that critical time, I simply persisted, learned, and experimented.

Perhaps the most challenging aspect of this business model is that you may not have compelling results for a few months. However, it leads to the most rewarding aspect of the model - notice that Google is propelling this article forward with no additional effort on my part. I don't know what the search volume ceiling looks like for this very niche article, but I believe this article will grow in month-over-month views for months to come.

Another result set I can share is what my first five months looked like in approximate Medium portfolio views:

Month 1 views: 100
Month 2 views: 2000
Month 3 views: 2500
Month 4 views: 4500
Month 5 views: 8200

In month 2 I had a few articles published in publications such as Better Programming and The Startup. Furthermore, my first month's articles escaped the "Google Sandbox". After month 2, I saw month-over-month growth of 25% to 80% which I expect to continue for years to come if I keep a consistent schedule publishing schedule.

The most interesting thing is that I published only two articles each in month 4 and month 5 (I was focused on writing eBooks instead). However, the wave of organic Google search traffic was swelling and pushing my business forward.

This business creates assets that generate passive income for months or years. I believe the more assets you create, the more your existing assets will generate. However, I also have seen that when I take a week (or three) off from Medium, the passive income continues to grow.

Publishing Cadence

If you want to gain momentum in building an internet business, I recommend publishing to Medium at least once a week. I also recommend creating at least two YouTube videos a month if you want to build a presence on YouTube. Finally, create at least one evergreen product (eBook, video course, etc.) to link to in your Medium articles and YouTube videos. However, do not lose sight of Medium as the hub, and make sure building out Medium gets at least 50% of your time.

Your results will naturally vary based on what you write about, how often you publish, and so on. However, I think there is some use in making assumptions and projecting what the future may look like. This can be highly motivating especially in the early stages of building your internet business.

If you follow a weekly publishing cadence and you gain the skill for writing articles that get 100 views per day, you can extrapolate revenue, monthly view count, and so on.

For example, after six months you would have 25 articles and 2500 views per day. If you see a 2% click-through rate to affiliate links, that is 50 clicks per day. If 10% of these clicks purchase your eBook or other premium product you linked to, that would be five sales per days. These numbers are roughly the percentages that I have experienced. Here is an estimate of the revenue from these numbers per day:

> 2500 views on Medium: $5 from Medium monetization
> 50 affiliate link clicks @ $0.05 per click: $2.50
> 5 sales per day @ $5 net royalty: $25
>
> Total: $32.50 daily, or about $1,000 per month

This is the possibility of a hub-and-spoke internet business model centered around Medium articles and organic Google traffic. There are limitless additional ways to add rocket fuel to your business's growth. Regardless of your results, you will certainly become a better software developer. Your business also will have unlimited potential in helping you find a new job, make new connections in the developer community, or fulfill whatever other goals you may have in your career.

Resources

James Altucher's Spoke and Wheel Model: https://jamesaltucher.com/blog/the-great-reset-part-2-the-spoke-and-wheel-model/

Amazon's affiliate commission schedule: https://affiliate-program.amazon.com/help/node/topic/GRXPHT8U84RAYDXZ

Override TextField Border Color for Different States in Material UI: https://medium.com/the-clever-dev/override-textfield-border-color-for-different-states-in-material-ui-2b61590d89ab?source=friends_link&sk=eb21fcc8134819222b33aecd388cbcb9

Intro to Material Table for React: https://medium.com/better-programming/intro-to-material-table-for-react-74db0fbd2d32?source=friends_link&sk=d722ef0e1b73a9958dd9c69b93435eb0

Intro to Material-UI Grid Component: https://medium.com/the-clever-dev/intro-to-material-ui-grid-component-ecc553a93200?sk=879e2454b20dc65e4ae6ce2e4747fc51

Material-UI Grid Align Items: https://medium.com/the-clever-dev/the-complete-guide-to-material-ui-grid-align-items-f4b472dba03f?source=friends_link&sk=31abb71c69a05c4660eacc3d85d2eb55

An Intro to Framer Motion: https://medium.com/better-programming/an-intro-to-framer-motion-fb37e732c4e9?source=friends_link&sk=bd1043109094610bd137c4c7ec56b1ab

Medium Enhanced Stats plugin – get more visibility into your Medium stats:

https://chrome.google.com/webstore/detail/medium-enhanced-stats/jnomnfoenpdinfkpaaigokicgcfkomjo?hl=en

A great site for tips on growing your internet business: https://fatstacksblog.com/ (and join the email list)

www.ingramcontent.com/pod-product-compliance
Lightning Source LLC
LaVergne TN
LVHW051618050326
832903LV00033B/4552